Black African Empires

by Joan Joseph

◄—A FIRST BOOK—►

FRANKLIN WATTS, INC. 1974

To my son, Robert Evan

Frontispiece:
A Benin bronze head of the Iyoba, the
queen mother. A sixteenth-century sculpture.
(The British Museum)

Illustration credits
THE BRITISH MUSEUM: pp. ii, viii,
3, 6A, 27, 44, 48, 52, 55, 56,
59, 60, 63, 68, 70A & B, 71B, 82, 86
RADIO TIMES HULTON PICTURE LIBRARY:
pp. 6B & C, 7A, B & C, 17,
34, 41, 71A, 77A & B
THE UNITED NATIONS: p. 13A

Cover by Terry Fehr
Map by Danmark & Michaels

Library of Congress Cataloging in Publication Data

Joseph, Joan.
    Black African empires.

    (A First Book)
    SUMMARY: Traces the rise and fall of
ancient African civilizations and their influence
on the development of the continent.
    Bibliography: p.
    1. Africa—History—To 1884—Juvenile lit-
erature. [1. Africa—History] I. Title.
DT25.J67   960′.2   73-14555
ISBN 0-531-00811-8

CONTENTS

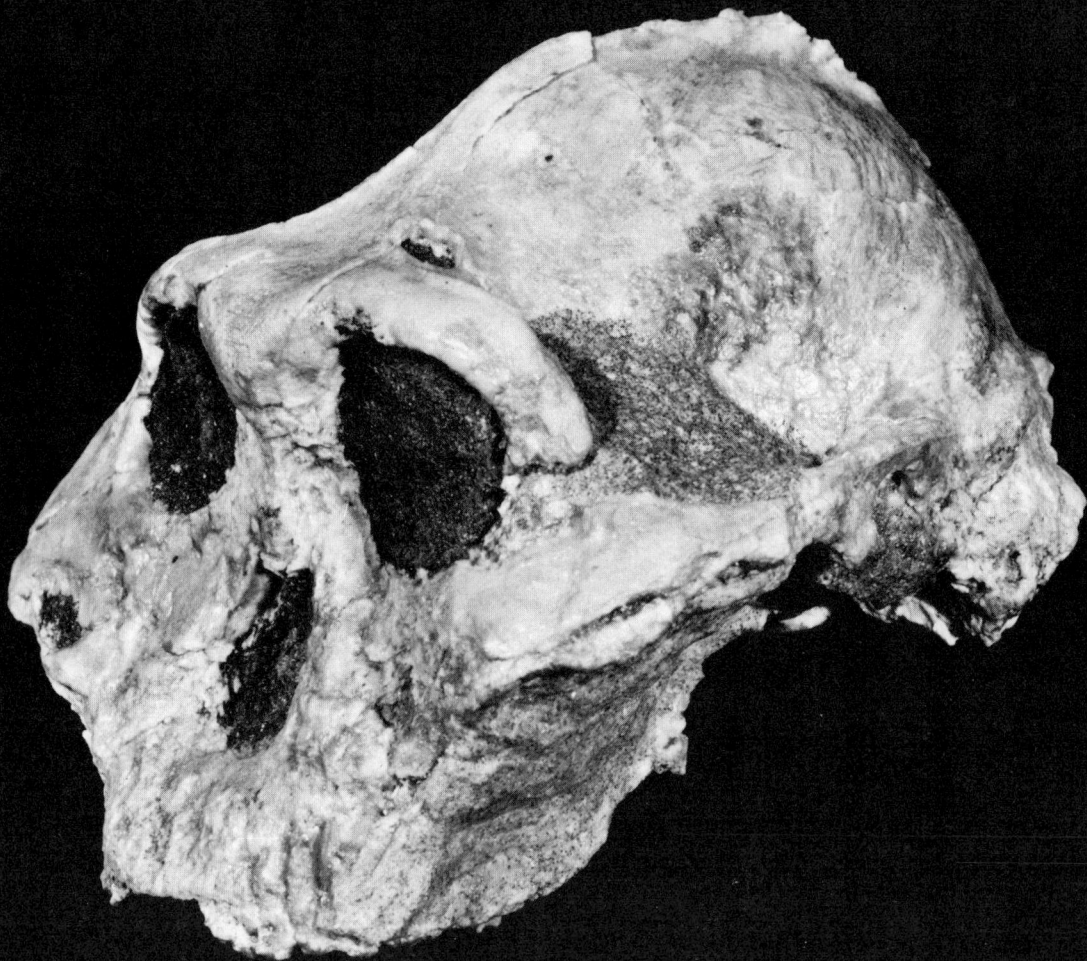

*A cast of the original
skull of Zinjanthropus.*

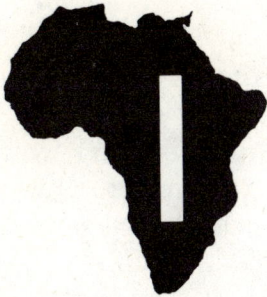

AFRICA, THE BIRTHPLACE OF MAN

The heritage of Africa is at last recognized by the world as including the earliest human development. More likely than not, Africa was the birthplace of man. Passing from the era of prehistory to the earliest periods of recorded history, the civilizations of ancient Africa, once called the "Dark Continent," shine brilliantly, proudly standing up to comparison with other ancient civilizations around the world. Today, however, Africa stands in the forefront, for she alone lays claim to possessing the secrets of the evolution of man. In the early history of Africa is the proof that there is a "brotherhood of all mankind."

For a long time, it was believed that Asia had been the home of our earliest ancestors. Then, in 1924, in a limestone quarry near the sands of the great Kalahari Desert, in Bechuanaland, South Africa, Professor Raymond A. Dart discovered a complete skull of a four- to five-year-old animal. Actually, it was a fossil skull—a skull that over hundreds of thousands of years had been preserved by chemical changes and converted to stone. "This child," as the professor referred to it, "looked amazingly human. The brain was so large and the face so human," he said, "that I was confident that here, indeed, was one of our early progenitors [ancestors] that had lived on the African continent; and as it had chosen the southern part of Africa for its homeland, I called it '*Australopithecus africanus,*' that is, the South African Ape."

Dart believed that the South African Ape, who had lived some five hundred thousand to one million years before, was the link in Darwin's theory of evolution, the link that proved without question that man had descended from prehuman creatures.

It was not until 1959, however, that scientists as a whole were convinced of Dart's theory. On July 17 of that year, in the deepest canyon of the Olduvai Gorge in Tanzania, Mary Leakey, an anthropologist married to Kenya-born anthropologist Dr. Louis Leakey, discovered a fossilized skull that was some 1,750,000 years old. The discovery of *Zinjanthropus*—the man of Zanj—as Dr. Leakey named this newly found specimen, was most exciting, for he was believed to be the direct ancestor of modern man. As the Leakeys continued digging in Bed I, the deepest and oldest soil of the gorge, they also found pebble tools. These pebbles, which had been chipped and sharpened to give them a cutting edge, are now believed to be the first evidence distinguishing man from his prehuman past. But the pebble tool culture of Dr. Leakey's "nutcracker man," as he is often called, was still not the last link in the chain of man's development. In 1961, at the bottom of Bed II, which dates back about a half million years, Dr. Leakey found hand axes. Fossil skulls were also found in Bed II, and this man was named "skillful man" or "*Homo habilis.*"

Then, on November 9, 1972, just one month and nine

Pebble tools found
in the Olduvai Gorge.

2

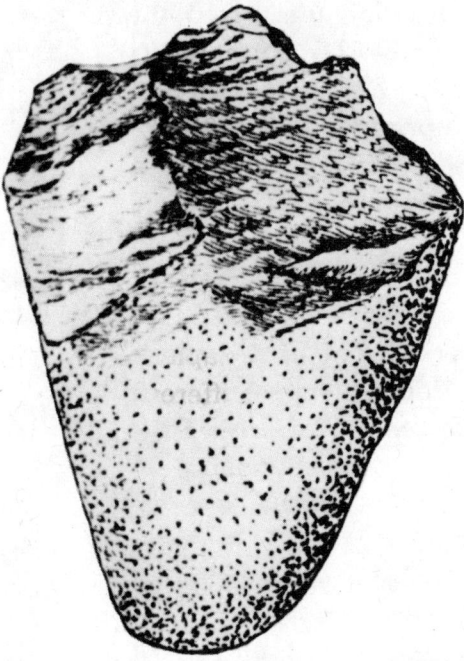

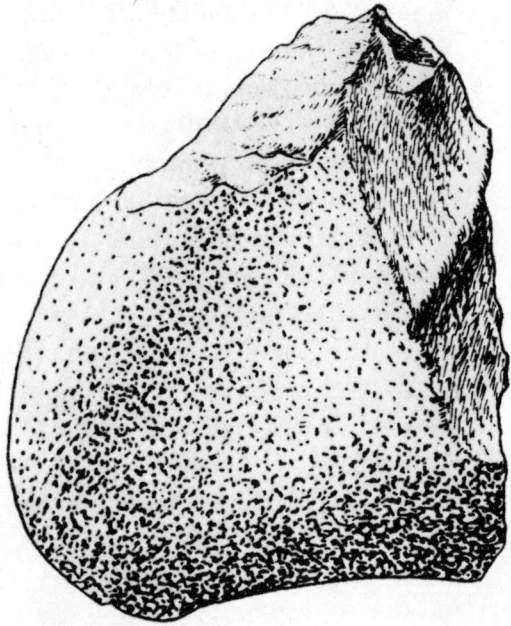

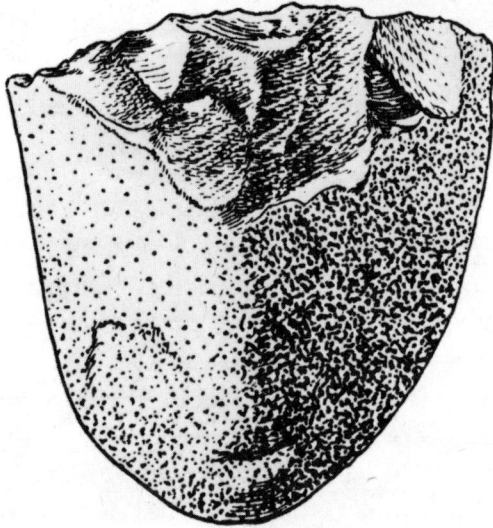

days after Dr. Leakey died, his son Richard uncovered the bones of a man, which are believed to be 2,600,000 years old. Examination of the thigh bones of this "near-man" indicated that he walked in a nearly upright position. These fossilized bones, found in the desert sands of northern Kenya, on the eastern shores of Lake Rudolf, have caused scientists to question the theory of human evolution. Until this revolutionary find, most scientists accepted Darwin's theory that man evolved, over hundreds of thousands of years, from apelike ancestors; they agreed that in the course of time, changes in environment had caused our earliest ancestors, *Australopithecus,* to abandon their tree dwellings and descend to the ground where a greater abundance of food was available. "Upright man," *Homo erectus,* was believed to have evolved some 500,000 years later; and another half million years was said to have elapsed before modern man, *Homo sapiens,* came into being.

But now Richard Leakey's new discovery had caused some to question the belief that there was a gradual process of evolution that did not give birth to true *Homo sapiens* until some 75,000 years ago. "While the skull is different from our own species, *'Homo sapiens,'*" Leakey stated when he reported his find, "it is also different from all other known forms of early man and thus does not fit into any of the presently held theories of human evolution. . . . The whole shape of the brain case is remarkably reminiscent of modern man, lacking the heavy and protruding eyebrow ridges and thick bone that are characteristic of *'Homo erectus'* known from young deposits in both Africa and Asia." The thigh bones that were found, he explained, "have astounded anatomists and other scientists because they are practically undistinguishable from the same bones of modern man." He

4

also stated that the hand bones that were examined confirmed that this man may well have been capable of using his hands almost, if not as skillfully, as modern man.

Further challenging Darwin's theory, Richard Leakey declared that in his opinion the skull and thigh bones he had unearthed presented "clear evidence" that more than two and a half million years ago, at the same time as "near-man" lived in South Africa, a large brained, "truly upright . . . form of man," who walked as we do rather than with a loping gait, lived in East Africa.

Future digs may push man's origins back even further, and the story of the birth of man may be rewritten again and again. Discoveries to date indicate that our earliest ancestors made their home somewhere in the Great Rift valley of East Africa, but even with this newest find, the puzzling question of man's origin still remains unanswered.

As man developed, he began to roam across ancient Africa. Today, most anthropologists believe that just as he adapted his needs to his environment, so did his skin coloring adapt to the climatic conditions where he settled. Today, the Mediterranean peoples in North Africa, living in a semi-tropical climate, have a far lighter skin color than the people who have made their home under the tropical sun of the great open savannas of western Africa. Along with the climatic reason, the lighter complexion of the Mediterranean peoples is caused by the mixture of Negro and Caucasian races.

The West African people, the darkest-skinned peoples of the continent, are believed to be the "true Negroes" of Africa. The Pygmies, thought to be among the earliest inhabitants of Africa, live in the rain forests of western and

THE PEOPLES OF AFRICA:
*Left: Ugandans, Above Right: a
chief of the Mandara tribe of Bornu,
Below Right: a Somalian.*

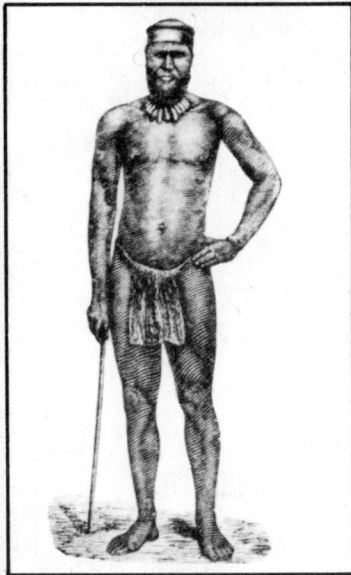

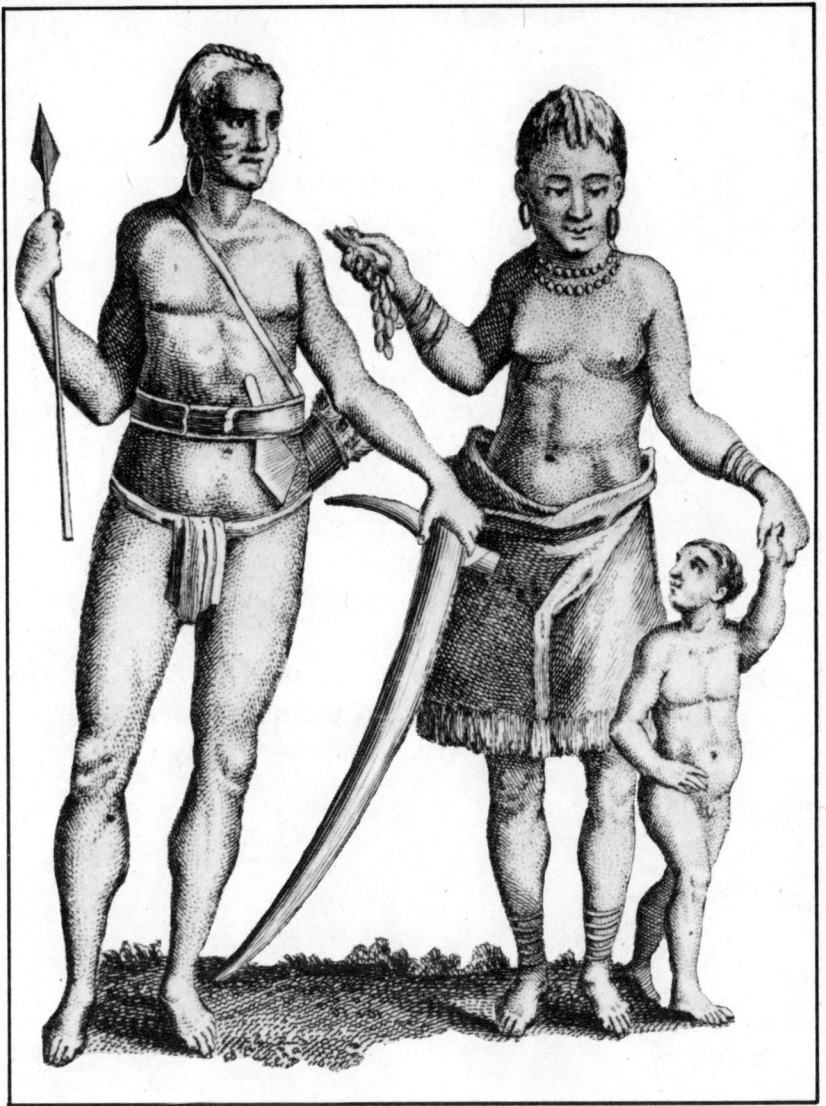

Above Left: a Bushman,
Below Left: a Zulu,
and Right: inhabitants
of the Gold Coast.

central Africa. It is held that their skin coloring is lighter than their Negro cousins in that they are protected from the direct rays of the sun by the thick foliage of the jungles. The Bushmen of the Kalahari Desert are also believed to have been among the earliest inhabitants of Africa, but their origins are still uncertain.

On the east coast of Africa live the Hamites. These people are spoken of in the Bible as the descendants of Ham, the son of Noah. Their skin is a yellowish brown and their features are far more similar to the Mediterranean peoples than to those of the rest of Africa. There is some question as to whether they came from Asia or developed in Africa, but regardless of where the Hamites originated, their culture was African.

Africa, therefore, is composed of many peoples whose fascinating history and cultural development are the result of their varied origins and contrasting environments.

2

CONTINENT
OF CONTRASTS

If the deserts of Africa were combined, the whole of the United States, an area of about three and a half million square miles, could be set into the center and it still would be surrounded by one million square miles of desert.

The continent of Africa did not always have four and a half million square miles of desert. Four to five thousand years ago, the great Sahara region contained a small desert surrounded by a rich, fertile woodland, blooming with vegetation and abounding with fish and game. Then, climatic changes occurred: the rivers dried up and the verdant grasses wilted away; the fish died and the animals wandered to more hospitable areas. The people of Africa north of the Sahara were cut off from those south of the barren mass of sand. In many ways they severed ties with each other, and their cultures, therefore, developed along very different lines. Egypt, looking out onto the Mediterranean Sea, flourished and her great civilization was accessible to the European world. At the same time, however, there were also great civilizations flourishing in other parts of Africa, but the thirteen-hundred-mile wall of the Sahara, stretching endlessly from the waters of the Atlantic to those of the Red Sea, concealed the developments in the south.

Africa's geographical conditions not only drew an imaginary line across sub-Saharan Africa, but also decreased the

African Empires

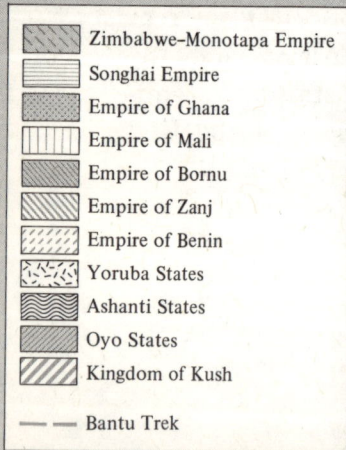

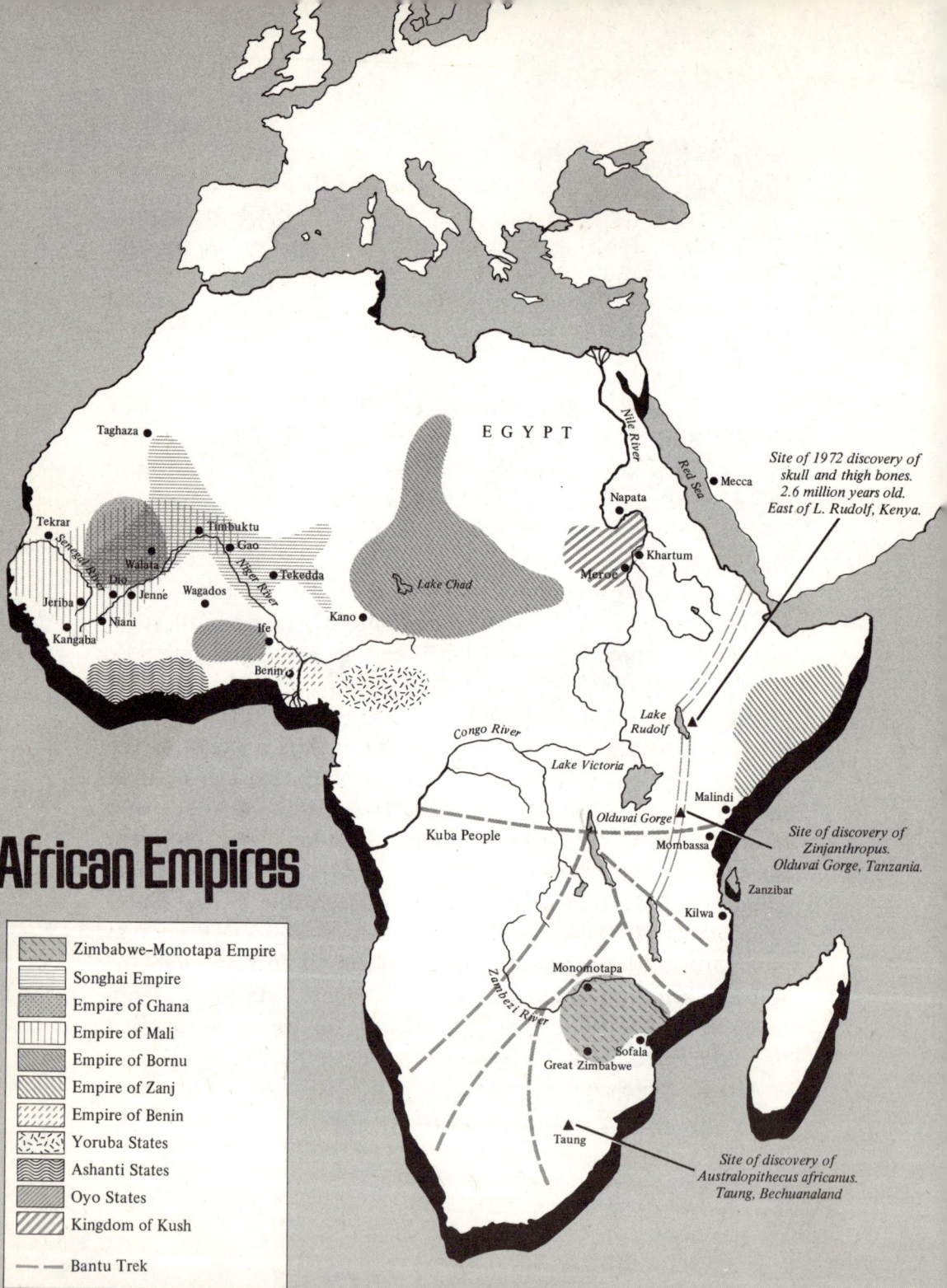

Labels on map:

EGYPT

Taghaza

Site of 1972 discovery of skull and thigh bones. 2.6 million years old. East of L. Rudolf, Kenya.

Mecca

Napata

Tekrar

Senegal River

Timbuktu

Gao

Walata

Dio

Tekedda

Khartum

Meroe

Jeriba

Jenne

Wagados

Niani

Niger River

Kangaba

Ife

Kano

Lake Chad

Benin

Congo River

Lake Victoria

Lake Rudolf

Kuba People

Olduvai Gorge

Malindi

Mombassa

Site of discovery of Zinjanthropus. Olduvai Gorge, Tanzania.

Zanzibar

Kilwa

Zambezi River

Monomotapa

Great Zimbabwe

Sofala

Taung

Site of discovery of Australopithecus africanus. Taung, Bechuanaland

Nile River

Red Sea

Legend:

- Zimbabwe-Monotapa Empire
- Songhai Empire
- Empire of Ghana
- Empire of Mali
- Empire of Bornu
- Empire of Zanj
- Empire of Benin
- Yoruba States
- Ashanti States
- Oyo States
- Kingdom of Kush
- — — Bantu Trek

opportunities for interchange among the peoples in different areas. The cattle owners of the scorched savannas of the Sudan became a nomadic people, constantly in search of new grazing land; the coastal peoples of East Africa were strongly influenced by their contacts with Arab and Asian traders, whereas the more inland groups had only limited contacts with others.

Millions of years ago, volcanic activity caused a great canyon to be formed in eastern Africa. The Great Rift valley, as it is called, carved its way from the northern borders of modern Kenya southward through Tanzania and into Mozambique. The Great Rift, at places forty miles wide and over two thousand feet deep, is one of the most fertile areas of Africa. It was, therefore, ideal for the home of a pastoral people and is believed to have been the birthplace of man, for the Olduvai Gorge, where *Zinjanthropus* was found, is a canyon in the Great Rift valley.

The Nile River, flowing north from the heart of the African continent to the Mediterranean, would appear to be a natural highway between the peoples settled in the lands south of the Sahara and those of the north. But the southern part of the river, in the southern Sudan, is an impenetrable swamp, a screen of tangled weeds known as the Sudd. The Sudd acted as another wall preventing contact between the civilizations of the south and those of the north.

The Negroes along the west coast of Africa have been in contact with Arab traders for centuries; though their civili-

Over: AREAS OF AFRICA:
The Matmata Mountains near Lybia,
a forest of the southern Sudan, and
Lake Nyasa on the border of Mozambique.

11

zations were influenced by the Arabs, they were in no way patterned after the Muslim world. But both Negroes and Arabs were virtually unable to penetrate the tropical rain forests along the Guinea Coast, and so the tribal life of the Pygmies developed along completely different lines.

The growth of the population was also determined by climate. The damp and swampy lands of Africa's equatorial rain forests are a perfect breeding ground for insects carrying diseases such as yellow fever and a haven for the malaria mosquito and the tsetse fly: a vicious insect whose deadly bite infected man and beast alike with sleeping sickness. In these regions, therefore, the population increased slowly and the high death toll from disease acted as a natural barrier, isolating these peoples from outside influence.

Cut off from the Mediterranean world, the great civilizations of Africa developed primarily along the coastal areas and in the steppes of central Africa where there was fertile soil and meadow land.

This then is the land of Africa—a land of contrasts, ranging from the marshes of the rain forests to the snows of Kilimanjaro; from the parched, sunbaked sands of the Sahara and the Kalahari to the lush greenery of the Great Rift valley. And in this land of many peoples, speaking hundreds of different dialects, great empires arose.

THE KINGDOM
OF KUSH

Out of the misty haze that blurs the historical outline of man's earliest beginnings in Africa, rises one of the greatest centers of the ancient world—the kingdom of Kush.

The earliest history of Kush dates back to the Book of Genesis, in which Noah's three sons are described as the founders of the nations of the world. But there have been no records found, as yet, describing Kush prior to the third millennium B.C., although it is believed that the Kushites began as a simple community of hunters and fishermen who had settled along the swampy banks of the middle Nile.

From about 3000 B.C. to 2200 B.C., "the land of Kush," as the Egyptians called the area that lay to the south of their frontier, was under Egyptian domination. Egyptian pharaohs constructed forts and established trading posts as well as centers of worship to their gods. Then, sometime around 1570 B.C., they occupied the area and annexed it to their kingdom. Under the rule of the pharaohs, the Kushites prospered. Their land was important to Egypt; it was a rich source of gold and ebony and their countrymen were sought after both as soldiers and slaves.

By 750 B.C., the Kushites had gained such wealth and power that they were ready to rise above their conquerors. Under the leadership of Kashta, their first great king, the Kushite army marched against Egypt, but the conquest was not completed until 725 B.C., when Kashta's son Piankhi became the first Kushite of the twenty-fifth dynasty of pharaohs, popularly known as the Ethiopian dynasty.

The pharaohs of the Ethiopian dynasty ruled over one of the greatest kingdoms of the ancient world. Their lands stretched from the shores of the Mediterranean to the borders of modern Ethiopia; they controlled Upper and Lower Egypt, and 1,400 miles of the great Nile River ran through their kingdom. Ruled by Kushites, the kingdom developed further as a great cultural center. The pottery of Kush has been said to "rank with the finest products of ceramic art of the ancient world"; their craftsmen designed exquisite jewelry, and ivory from Kush was used to decorate palaces as far afield as Persia; there is even evidence that an established trade existed between the kingdom of Kush and the Han dynasty of China.

Sometime around 530 B.C., the Kushites moved their capital south from Napata to Meroë, which was about 120 miles north of present-day Khartoum. Meroë was one of the great ironworking cities of ancient times. It was a center for smelting, and the methods used by its smiths to fashion iron weapons and utensils are believed to have spread throughout Africa. Meroë, which developed into a large city with imposing palaces and temples, remained the capital of Kush for eight hundred years. In many ways it resembled the major cities of Egypt. Kushite pharaohs wore the two-tiered crown symbolizing the unity of Upper and Lower Egypt; their ruling families, when they died, were buried in pyramids, built more than eight centuries after the last royal pyramid had been erected in Egypt; Kushite temples were

The pyramids of Meroë.

16

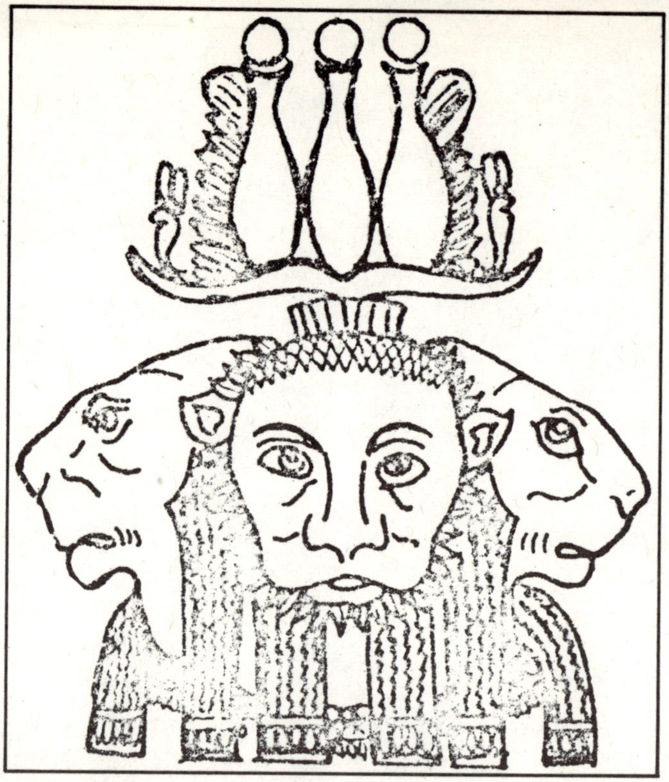

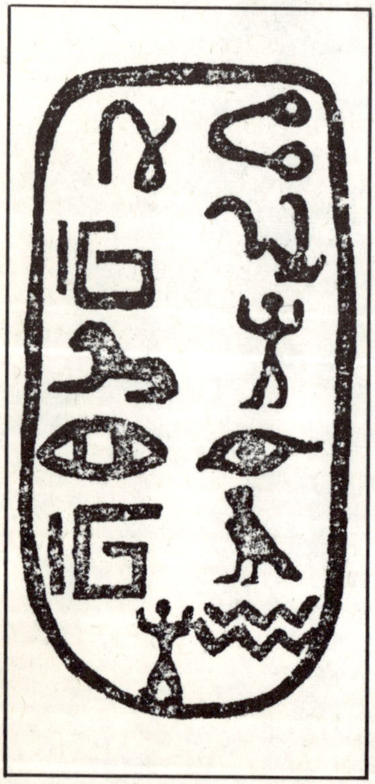

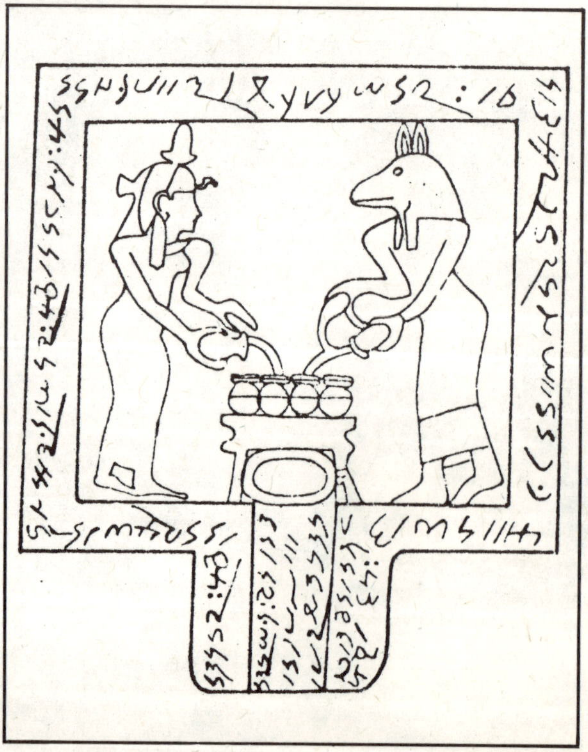

patterned after those of Egypt, and Egyptian gods, such as the sun god, Amon-re, were worshiped as Kushite gods.

But although the people of Kush absorbed Egyptian culture, they retained their own identity. One distinct trait was that the Kushites worshiped their own king. (Belief in the divinity of kings played a major role in the development of many of the kingdoms of Africa.) Meroë, a great trading center, was also influenced by other cultures. The chief god of the Kushites, the lion god Apedemak, is depicted as having three heads and four arms, a representation that strongly suggests an Indian influence. A further example is seen in the system of reservoirs in Meroë, which appear to have been patterned after those of the Arabs living on the eastern shores of the Red Sea.

At the time of Egyptian dominance, it is known that the Kushites adopted their conquerors' form of hieroglyphic writing, but as close contact with Egypt lessened and Kush became independent, Kushite scribes developed their own form of writing. They created their own Meroitic hieroglyphs, and in time advanced to writing in "Meroitic cursive script." Modern scholars have succeeded in deciphering the sounds of this twenty-three-symbol alphabet and are able to read the words, but, to date, no one has found the key to understanding the script. Historical knowledge of the important events that occurred after the capital of Kush was moved to Meroë is, therefore, very limited.

Meroitic reliefs that have been unearthed indicate that in

Above: The lion god Apedemak.
Below Left: Meroitic hieroglyphs.
Below Right: An offering table
showing Meroitic cursive script.

19

the latter years of the kingdom, the Kushites were continually at war, desperately trying to push back the nomadic desert peoples that were invading their land. But their days of glory were past. A new and powerful kingdom was rising in northern Ethiopia. Axum, known in biblical times as the birthplace of the Queen of Sheba, was expanding her boundaries and Ezna, the king of Axum, set his sight on the land of Kush. In A.D. 325, Ezna invaded Meroë and was crowned "king of Kush." The title was a meaningless one. The land of the Kushites had been destroyed, and with it a thousand years of history was virtually erased. It is only in very recent years that Kush has regained its place in history as the first truly African civilization, and as a kingdom that left its mark on both the Mediterranean and African worlds.

4 THE LAND OF GOLD (GHANA—THE SONINKE PEOPLE)

While the kingdom of Kush, on the eastern side of the continent, was fading out of the spotlight of history, the empire of Ghana, on the opposite side of the continent, was rising to the fore. The ancient empire of Ghana, which reached the height of its glory during the tenth and eleventh centuries A.D., should not be confused with the modern state that lies some one thousand miles to the southeast.

We know little about the early history of ancient Ghana, and our only real clues to the origin of its Soninke people are from the legendary stories, handed down from generation to generation, which the modern Soninke still tell. It is believed, however, that in the early years of the fourth century A.D., the Soninkes, who had settled in the valley between the banks of the Senegal River on the west and the bend of the Niger on the east, were invaded by nomadic tribes from North Africa. These desert warriors, known as Berbers, settled among their captives and adopted the Mande language of the Soninke; it is these Berbers who are thought to have been the actual founders of the first great empire of the western Sudan. The Berbers and Soninke called their kingdom Wagadou, after the royal clan of Wagadou, the rulers traditionally considered the founders of their kingdom; but their land became known as Ghana, the Mande word for war chief.

Sometime during the eighth century, Arab forces attempted to conquer Ghana. Though unsuccessful, their raids had two significant results: for the first time Muslim historians, geographers, and travelers began to take an interest in "the land of gold"; furthermore, Muslim travelers settled in Ghana, bringing with them their traditions of scholarship and spreading the ways of Islam to the Soninkes.

By the time of the Arab invasion, Ghana was a rich and powerful empire. Its influence was felt over the greater part of western Africa from modern Senegal and Gambia in the west to Lake Chad on the eastern borders of Nigeria; its control reached as far north as the wastelands of the Sahara and stretched south to the Gulf of Guinea.

In the twelfth century, Muslim historians claimed that the Soninkes had risen to their powerful position because they had iron weapons, while the tribes they invaded were still fighting with bars of black ebony wood. But there were other reasons that Ghana became such a great empire. For a thousand years Ghana's "Kayamaghan"—king of gold— was master of the trans-Saharan gold-salt trade. This was the lifeblood of the empire.

The boundaries of Ghana did not extend to the salt mines of Taghaza, but the king controlled this desolate village, which lay north of Timbuktu on the southern borders of modern Algeria. Even after the strength of Ghana's empire began to weaken, the salt mines at Taghaza remained important. In the fourteenth century an Arab traveler, Ibn Battuta, described Taghaza as "an unattractive village, with the curious feature that its houses and mosques are built of blocks of salt and roofed with camel skins. There are no trees there, nothing but sand; they dig for the salt and find it in thick slabs." And three hundred years earlier, in the

22

eleventh century—when the empire of Ghana was at the height of its glory—Taghaza was much like Ibn Battuta's later description; its only inhabitants were the slaves who mined the salt.

From the tenth century, if not earlier, the kings of Ghana recognized the importance of Taghaza. They knew that the people of Wangara, living to the south of their kingdom, had a desperate need for salt; it was a vital commodity, for it was the only means they had to replenish the loss of salt from their bodies due to the intense heat of the savanna zone in which they lived. It was this craving for salt that made them willing to sell a pound of gold for an equal quantity of salt.

The people from Wangara carried on their trade in strict secrecy and their method of silent or dumb bartering was quite extraordinary. They chose a special trading site on the banks of a river where merchants from Ghana brought salt and other articles, such as animal skins, ivory, kola nuts, and cotton. Each trader would place his salt bars in a row and pile his goods neatly behind the salt. When all the traders were ready, they would beat their "debas," long, hollowed wood drums, to announce that their market was open; then they would pull back a half day's journey from the marketplace.

The following morning the Wangara miners would arrive by boat. They would decide how much gold the merchandise was worth, leave the amount beside the appropriate pile, and disappear. Then the Ghanaians returned; it was up to them to determine if the amount of gold left was satisfactory. If the miners had not left enough gold, they would leave the piles exactly as they were, and once again they would pull back their caravans. They hoped, of course, that when the miners saw that the deal had not been completed, they would leave more gold. As soon as the merchants felt that the miners had left enough gold, they would beat their debas to signal that the trade had been completed. Through this manner of trading, the whereabouts of the Wangara gold fields were successfully concealed. Today, however, geological findings suggest that the mines of Wangara lay southwest of Ghana, between the Senegal and Faleme rivers.

5

THE LEGEND OF WAGADOU-BIDA (THE DOWNFALL OF GHANA)

The Soninkes had called their kingdom Wagadou, after their first rulers, but according to some legends they named their kingdom in honor of Wagadou-Bida, their protecting spirit and highest god. Wagadou was a great snake with many magical powers, and the Soninkes believed that he was responsible for their kingdom's wealth and prosperity.

In the middle of the eleventh century, when the empire of Ghana was at its height, it had two capitals: the walled city of El Ghaba, where the king lived, and the commercial center of Koumbi.

Koumbi was a bustling city, crowded with Arab merchants. Its market was the busiest in West Africa, for besides the trade in gold and salt, Koumbi supported one of the largest slave markets along the trans-Saharan caravan route. The slaves were captured from the weaker kingdoms that lay to the south of Ghana. Within the market, gold dust was used for the purchase of cattle, sheep, wheat, raisins, dried fruits, ivory, and pearls. In front of the market stalls sat ironsmiths who made weapons for the king's army; goldsmiths and coppersmiths could be seen making jewelry; there were cloth weavers, potters, and sandal makers; there were also leather tanners and craftsmen, and interestingly enough, the famous Moroccan leather goods actually originated in the medieval empire of Ghana.

El Ghaba was some six to ten miles away, and although the cities were completely different from one another, they were called the twin cities, for they were connected by a long line of small wooden and clay houses. The Arab writer El Bakri vividly described the king's city: "In the town where the king lives, and not far from the hall where he holds his court of justice, is a mosque where pray the Muslims who come on visiting diplomatic missions. Around the king's town are domed buildings, woods and copses where live the sorcerers of the people, the men in charge of the religious cult. In these also are idols and the tombs of their kings. These woods are guarded and no unauthorized person can enter them, so that it is not known what is within them. In them also are the prisons of the king, and if anyone is imprisoned there, no more is ever heard of him. The king's interpreters, his treasurer, and the majority of his ministers, are Muslims."

The woods described by El Bakri were sacred to the Soninke. Though many had converted to the faith of Islam, they still clung to their ancient traditions. They called the woods the "Sacred Grove," and it would probably have been impossible to find a Soninke who did not believe that the great snake Wagadou-Bida lived in a dark cave within the grove. The priests of Wagadou-Bida guarded the Sacred Grove twenty-four hours a day; they feared some nonbeliever would come into the grove and displease the holy snake. The king of Ghana himself was allowed to enter the grove only once during his lifetime—on the day he was crowned king. To pay homage to the holy snake, the Soninkes held an annual beauty contest throughout the empire. The young maiden who won the contest was sacrificed within the grove.

Wagadou-Bida, the sacred snake. A Yoruba carving.

The Soninkes not only believed that Wagadou-Bida protected their empire, but also claimed that the slaying of their holy snake was the cause of their country's downfall. According to the legends of the Soninke, in the year 1240, Sia, a girl from Koumbi, won the annual beauty contest in the empire. In true Soninke tradition, she was taken to the Sacred Grove where she was to have the honor of being sacrificed to Wagadou-Bida. But Sia was engaged to a great warrior by the name of Amadou, and Amadou was unwilling to accept his people's barbaric custom.

On the day chosen for the sacrifice, Amadou secretly entered the grove and hid behind a tree. When the great serpent came out of his cave, Amadou swiftly drew his sword and, in a flash, thrust his shining blade across the neck of the holy snake. But instead of falling to the ground, Wagadou's head flew through the air and landed in faraway Bambuk, an area that immediately became rich with gold. Much to Amadou's surprise, Wagadou-Bida was not dead; he had regrown his head. Again, Amadou viciously slashed the serpent's neck, and again Wagadou's head flew through the air; this time it landed in Bure, and here, too, the town was suddenly filled with gold. And still Wagadou was not dead. Amadou had to cut off the mighty serpent's head seven times before Wagadou-Bida was willing to accept defeat. As soon as the snake collapsed, the fearless warrior mounted his horse, snatched his beautiful bride-to-be, and rode away, never to be seen again.

The Soninke people wept for days; they knew that with Wagadou-Bida's death, their kingdom was doomed. Their priests used every curse they knew to bring harm to Amadou; they prayed continually, hoping to bring Wagadou-Bida back to life. But the great serpent did not return to life; in his absence, drought afflicted their kingdom. Their fertile lands dried up and their animals died of thirst. Fearing what else might happen, the Soninke fled from Ghana and became wandering nomads. And so, according to the legend, with the death of Wagadou-Bida, the great medieval empire of Ghana came to an end.

The legend of the slaying of Wagadou-Bida is a colorful one, but the true facts of Ghana's downfall are a matter of recorded history. At the beginning of the eleventh century, Ghana was at the height of its glory. Its power extended over a vast territory; its army had a reserve force of some 200,000 warriors, and its king was so wealthy that he used a gold nugget as a hitching post. But before the century ended, the empire began to crumble.

In 1042, a group of fanatic Muslims founded a sect known as the Almoravids. Like the Christian crusaders, the Almoravids were determined to convert the pagan peoples of Africa. In 1054 they stormed the commercial capital of Ghana; but Koumbi was a strong city and did not surrender for twenty-two years. With the fall of Koumbi, Ghana submitted to Almoravid rule. In 1087, Ghana regained her independence, and the Sisse clan of the Soninkes returned to the throne. But the damage was done; the empire was no longer a strong unified kingdom. During the next hundred years, its kings tried desperately to restore Ghana to its former status, but they were unsuccessful. In 1203 a neighboring tribe, the Susu, invaded and captured Ghana. The king was stripped of all his power, the entire Soninke population was enslaved, and the first of the great medieval empires of the western Sudan came to an end.

6

THE MURDER OF ELEVEN BROTHERS (MALI—THE MANDINKE PEOPLE)

Sumanguru, the Susu king who had conquered Koumbi, the commercial capital of Ghana, was hated by the Soninkes. His harsh rule and heavy system of taxation also caused a mass exodus of the Muslim merchants and traders from Koumbi to the northern town of Walata. Walata was beyond the reach of Sumanguru's powerful army and outside the territory he controlled. As a result, the commercial activity of Koumbi virtually came to a standstill and the trade upon which Ghana's greatness had been built was seriously hampered.

During Sumanguru's thirty-two-year rule, he succeeded in conquering the neighboring Mandingo people. The annexation of their kingdom of Kangaba, however, did little to strengthen his position. Deprived of trade, Sumanguru could do little to hold his empire together.

The Mandingo people were a serious threat to Sumanguru. They were a united group, not willing to be governed by a cruel ruler. Furthermore, they were rapidly extending their own territory, pushing their boundaries farther and farther to the south and southeast.

Fearing the growing power of the Mandingos, Sumanguru arranged for the assassination of the eleven brothers who were heirs to the throne of Kangaba. But as ruthless as the murders were, according to legend, the Susu king took pity on Sundiata, the youngest of the brothers. Some said Sundiata's life was spared because he was a sickly cripple who could not possibly have been a threat to Sumanguru; others claimed that he was in exile at the time of the murder of his brothers. According to others still, his very name possessed a magical power; *Sundiata* is the Mandinke word for "hungering lion." Some people believed it was his name that gave Sundiata the determination to bring back the strength in his legs. But whichever legend merits a place in history, the facts are indisputable. By 1235, Sundiata had not only learned to walk and become a skilled horseman, but also had amassed sufficient power to lead an army against Sumanguru's troops. The "hungering lion" merited his name. He succeeded in killing Sumanguru, conquering the Susu people, and annexing the area of the former empire of Ghana to his own kingdom.

When Sundiata came to the throne, Jeriba was the capital of Kangaba. With the annexation of Ghana, however, he felt that Niani, also situated along the Niger River, would be a far more central site from which to rule his kingdom. Sundiata moved to Niani and the Mandinke word *Mali,* meaning "where the king lives," became the name of his newly founded empire.

Like the Soninkes and the Susu, the Mandinke were a branch of the same family group of Mande-speaking peoples. But the Mandinke differed in one major way from their tribal brothers: they had accepted the Almoravid teachings and had willingly converted to the Islamic faith. This was of significant importance, for in that Sundiata was a devout Muslim, it was an easy task for him to reestablish contact with the Muslim merchants and traders who had moved to Walata.

Sundiata was an authoritative ruler and directed a most powerful army. In 1240, he sacked Koumbi, and in so doing he completed his conquest of Ghana and ended the brief rule of the Susu kings.

In the latter years of his life, Sundiata proceeded to establish peace within his land and to develop the economy of his country. He encouraged agriculture and the cultivation of new crops, such as cotton, which greatly enriched his empire. In 1255, Sundiata suddenly and mysteriously died. But he had set the stage; he had built the foundations of the second of the great medieval empires of the western Sudan.

7

MANSA MUSA, THE BLACK MOSES (THE EMPIRE OF MALI)

The empire of Mali grew to be even greater than Ghana. Under Sundiata, medieval Mali covered much the same territory as the modern state of the same name. When Sundiata's son Uli became king, however, the empire expanded in all directions.

Uli, like his father, was a devout Muslim and his religious convictions were so deep that he insisted upon making the holy pilgrimage to Mecca. The "hajj," as the pilgrimage is called, was an important trip—in addition to its religious purpose, the hajj established a trade route to the Arabian peninsula. The pilgrimage became a tradition that was followed by almost every succeeding ruler of the medieval Malian Empire.

Upon Uli's death, in 1270, his brother Karifa ascended the throne. Karifa was a strange king, for he was apparently completely insane. To this day, the Mande-speaking tribes of West Africa tell stories of how Karifa amused himself by shooting arrows at the people in his courtyard.

Karifa's short reign, the exact dates of which are uncertain, began a period of unrest within the kingdom. During the next forty years, one incompetent ruler after another sat on the throne. It was not until 1307, when Mansa Kankan Musa, the grandson of one of Sundiata's sisters, came to the throne, that the empire again began to flourish.

The city of Timbuktu.

Musa, the Arabic word for Moses, was more than just the emperor of Mali. To the Mandinke, Musa, the most remarkable monarch of the Sudan, was unquestionably the "Black Moses"; they believed he had been sent by Allah to build Mali into the greatest empire of the medieval world. And Mansa Musa did just that.

Ghana had controlled the trans sub-Saharan salt-gold trade. Musa stretched his lands west to the Atlantic coast and north to include the salt mines of Taghaza; in the south, his borders encircled the fabled lands of Wangara and Bambuk; and in the east, he gained control of the copper mines —the most important source of his kingdom's wealth—of Takedda.

Al Omari, an Arab historian of the time, described Musa as: "The most important of the Moslem Negro kings; he is the king who is the most powerful, the richest, the most fortunate, the most feared by his enemies and the most able to do good to those around him."

Mansa Musa not only brought peace and prosperity to his empire, but also made it into one of the great cultural and educational centers of the world. Timbuktu, on the northern banks of the Niger River, became a great center of commerce, religion, and scholarship. Lawyers, doctors, theologians, and scholars from all over the Arab world congregated in this important seat of learning to study at the renowned University of Sankoré.

Under Musa, the kingdom of Mali won wide recognition, and, therefore, when he made his pilgrimage to Mecca, it attracted the attention of numerous writers. The caravans that accompanied Musa are said to have been lavishly outfitted, but the details of his long journey are too camouflaged by legendary tales to permit the true facts to be learned.

But even without an accurate description of the hajj, there is no question that the sensational trip became an event of such importance throughout the Muslim world that Mansa Musa became known as the lord of Mali and the khan of Africa. Artists began portraying the Black Moses with flowing gowns, crowned in gold and, in most stately fashion, holding up his golden orb and scepter. Writers of the period praised his justice and marveled at the peace and security within his vast kingdom. In his *Travels in Asia and Africa, 1324–1354*, Ibn Battuta gives a vivid picture of the empire in the later years of Musa's reign: "There is complete security within their country. Neither traveler nor inhabitant in it has anything to fear from robbers or men of violence." Battuta, a devout Muslim, was most impressed that: "On Fridays, if a man does not go early to mosque, he cannot find a corner to pray in, on account of the crowd." Battuta's writings stress the cleanliness of the Mandinke people and the importance they placed on learning; but he was shocked by the fact that: "Women go naked in the Sultan's [Musa's] presence without even a veil; his daughters also go about naked . . . I saw about a hundred women slaves coming out of the Sultan's palace with food and they were naked."

Battuta did not understand the cultural heritage of the Mandinke; for though the emperor was a devout Muslim and some of his people followed the teachings of Islam, many did not and in any case they were not prepared to abandon their traditional way of life.

In 1337, the twenty-five-year reign of Mansa Kankan Musa came to an end, and with his death, the fabulous empire of Mali began to decay.

Mansa Musa's son Mansa Maghan did not have the capacity to follow in the steps of the great Black Moses. During Maghan's four-year reign, Mali suffered greatly. The important cultural center of Timbuktu was raided; the magnificent mosques and the palace of the city were set aflame, and much of Timbuktu was reduced to a mere bed of ashes.

The empire of Mali did not disappear overnight. In fact, it managed to survive another three hundred years, but during these three centuries its people were constantly at war with neighboring tribes. While the Songhai were rising in the east, Mali was being invaded by desert nomads from the north as well as by the southern Mossi living along the banks of the Upper Volta River.

Timbuktu had been the first to fall; then Walata was captured by a desert tribe known as the Tuaregs. Kingdoms like Tekrur and Songhai broke away from Mali, and the Mandinke people, lacking a strong ruler, watched the boundaries of their kingdom shrink. By the middle of the seventeenth century, the fabulous medieval empire of Mali came to an end. The circle had been completed; all that remained was Kangaba, the original state of the Mandingo people.

8

AN ARMY CROSSES
THE SAHARA DESERT
(THE SONGHAI EMPIRE)

The empires of Ghana and Mali had risen to great heights, but they could not compare to the Songhai Empire, the third great medieval power that ruled the central Sudan during the fifteenth and sixteenth centuries.

According to tradition, the Songhai were descendants of an ancient West African tribe that had settled along the banks of the middle Niger. Sometime between the seventh and ninth centuries, the Dia tribe of Berber nomads invaded and conquered the Songhai. Their chief, Za el Ayamen, became the first of the Za or Dia dynasty of kings.

Inscriptions that have been uncovered in recent years show that as early as 1010, the Dia king Kossi established his capital at Gao and made it the commercial center of the Songhai people. King Kossi accepted the teachings of Islam and, in so doing, he opened the door to trade with Muslim countries. Gao became a crossroads for caravans from Egypt and North Africa traveling to points south and west of the Songhai Empire. Muslim traders settled in Gao. This ever-growing commercial center attracted Muslim scholars, and Gao, like Timbuktu earlier, became a great seat of learning. The acceptance of Islam by the ruling class did not influence the people, who still held to their traditional beliefs and worshiped their tribal gods. Nevertheless, from the reign of

King Kossi on, it became an accepted custom that all Songhai rulers must be Muslim.

The rise of the Songhai Empire is traditionally said to have begun in 1010. Its growth continued steadily until 1325, when Gao was captured by the powerful Mansa Musa of Mali. During his memorable hajj, Musa had taken the two sons of King Dia Assibai as hostages. Throughout the ten years of their captivity, the princes, Ali Kolon and Sulayman Nar, appeared to be loyal supporters of Mansa Musa, but in reality they were systematically stealing arms and supplies from Mali's army. Following Musa's death, when the weak Maghan ascended the throne, their return to Gao was accomplished with ease.

King Dia Assibai had died while his sons were in Mali. Upon their return to Gao, Ali Kolon, the elder of the boys, claimed his right to the throne and became the first ruler of the Sunni or Replacement dynasty. Under the Sunni dynasty, the Songhai Empire became a powerful state. In 1400, Sunni Ma Doga, the Giant, attacked Mali and pillaged her capital. But it was not until the reign of Sunni Ali Ber—Ali the Great—that the Songhai Empire rose above the empire of Mali and became the most powerful kingdom in the central Sudan.

The reign of Ali the Great lasted from 1464 to 1492. During these years he proved to be a strong ruler and a fearless warrior. Some considered him a harsh tyrant, but he earned the respect of his people, who spoke of him as a god, calling him "the most high." The reputation of Ali the Great became a legend in the central Sudan, and even today, his name is remembered by the half million or more Songhai living in northwest Nigeria along the Niger River banks.

Just as Ali Ber was respected by his people, so was he hated and feared by his enemies. From the beginning of his reign, he ruled from the battlefield, taking his court on every campaign. He established the first professional fighting force known to the Sudan area and created a great navy—an important step in the success of his scheme to control the Great Bend of the Niger River. The Tuaregs, a desert people traditionally enemies of the Songhai, also sought to control the middle Niger. In 1433, they had invaded Mali and captured the great commercial city of Timbuktu. Ali Ber believed Timbuktu rightfully belonged to the Songhai Empire. Located at the curve of the Great Bend, its inhabitants were believed to be Songhai in origin. In 1468, Ali Ber led his army against the Tuaregs, plundering Timbuktu and slaughtering its citizens. Though he professed to follow the teachings of Islam, he had no sympathy for the Muslim traders or scholars of the city who had had any dealings with his enemies. His cruel treatment of the Muslim community was most bitterly described by unforgiving Muslim writers.

Having conquered Timbuktu, Ali Ber set his sights beyond the Great Bend of the Niger, 300 miles southwest to the town of Jenné. Jenné, founded in the thirteenth century by the Soninke of Ghana, was an important commercial center as well as a great seat of learning. Its university was one of the finest in the world and claimed to have over one thousand faculty members. Its medical school had an outstanding reputation, and doctors from Jenné were known to have performed difficult surgical operations with amazing success.

Jenné was considered an invincible city. The kings of Mali had tried to conquer it ninety-nine times, but then gave up in despair. The defeat of others, however, did not deter Ali Ber.

The city of Timbuktu.

It took him seven years, seven months, and seven days to complete his conquest. When he finally captured Jenné, in 1473, he did not pillage the town; instead, he married the young king's mother. A pledge of lasting friendship was taken by the two rulers and from that time on the kings of Jenné had the right to share the royal mat of the Songhai kings.

With the capture of Jenné, the Songhai Empire had become the most powerful state in the western Sudan. For the next twenty years, Ali Ber continued to push out the boundaries of his lands and maintained a strong central government. By the time of his death in 1492, he had established a stable empire.

Ali Ber was succeeded by his son, but the young king's rule only lasted about a year. In 1493, one of Ali Ber's own military advisers, Mohammed Touré, rebelled. Overthrowing the young ruler, he ascended the throne as the first of the Askia dynasty, and took that name.

Askia is usually considered the greatest of the Songhai kings. Not only did he build the largest and wealthiest kingdom in the Sudan, but also the Songhai Empire, under Askia, became the most highly organized kingdom in precolonial Africa. Askia established an efficient system of government. He appointed Islamic judges in every large district, and the law of Islam became the law of the land. Under Askia the Great, the Songhai Empire reached the peak of its glory.

But Askia's end was not in keeping with his achievements. When he was eighty years of age, one of his own sons led a revolt against him. Askia was exiled to an uninhabited island in the Niger River and it was not until his son was firmly in control that he was allowed to return to Gao. He died in 1538, a virtual prisoner in his own palace.

Askia's sons did not have the strength of their father and the great Songhai Empire began to totter. This was just what the rulers of Morocco had been waiting for. For a long time they had had their eyes on the commercial and cultural center of Songhai, but the endless sands of the Sahara had always been an effective deterrent to invasion. In 1589, however, El Mansur, the sultan of Morocco, decided to conquer Songhai. He sent an army of 4,000 soldiers, under the command of Judar Pasha, south to Gao. It took the army six months to cross the desert and even before they reached the Songhai capital 3,000 men had died. The remaining soldiers were exhausted, but they were armed with guns and gunpowder, while all the Songhai army had to fight back with were spears and swords.

Gao fell quickly and Timbuktu surrendered with hardly a fight. "From that moment everything changed," wrote a Songhai historian of the time, "danger took the place of security; poverty, of wealth. Peace gave way to distress, disasters, violence. . . ."

El Mansur died in 1603 and with him was buried Morocco's dream of controlling the gold mines of the Sudan. Following El Mansur's raid, the empire disintegrated rapidly, and with its decline, the last and greatest of the medieval empires of the western Sudan came to an end.

*Fishing on the River Shary
in the area around Lake Chad.*

9

AN ARISTOCRATIC ARMY
(THE EMPIRE OF BORNU)

A favorite legend still popular among the peoples of the central Sudan is that the land around Lake Chad was the home of the biblical Noah. The peoples living on the southwestern shores of the lake must have believed this story, for sometime before the twelfth century, they named their land Bornu, which means "the country of Noah." Furthermore, they called their dynasty the "Sefuwa"—the sons of Sef— for they claimed their rulers were the direct descendants of Adam's first-born son, Seth.

The So were believed to have migrated to Lake Chad sometime around the eighth century A.D. According to another legend, they were unusually tall people and thus had no difficulty conquering the "little men," occupying the area, and establishing themselves on the east bank of the lake. The So have disappeared, but archeologists have unearthed enough relics to permit us a glimpse into their way of life. They constructed towns and built houses in red brick—a building material presumably unknown elsewhere in Africa during this period. Their art appears to have been a combination of the cultures of the valley of the Nile and that of the Niger. They made rams' heads in pottery, resembling the Egyptian sun god, Amon-re; they worked in bronze and used the same "lost wax" method known in the Nile valley and later used by the artists of Ife and Benin.

Remains of their civilization unearthed to date suggest that the So were the link connecting the civilizations that rose from east to west along the great Sahara Desert's southern border.

As mysteriously as the So arrived, they disappeared. And though the magnitude of their civilization is still undetermined, the empire of Kanem-Bornu, which flourished following their disappearance, is well documented and is known to have been the longest lasting as well as the most colorful of the medieval empires of the Sudan.

With the arrival of the Kanuri people in the grassy flatlands of the Chad basin, a new period began in the history of the central Sudan. Sometime during the eighth century, the Sefuwa tribe appointed themselves the leaders of the Kanuri and laid the foundations of the powerful Kanemba Nation. Forming a tribal council of twelve members, the Sefuwa created a central government with such powers that the empire of Kanem was, in the words of a modern historian, "truly in the Middle Ages the civilizer of the central Sudan just as Mali, inheritor of Ghana, was the civilizer of the western Sudan. These were the centers which saw the elaboration of Sudanese civilization as we know it today; so different from the civilization of the Arabs and from the more purely Negro tribes of the south."

For much of Africa's early history, the principal sources of information for historians are the centuries-old tribal tales that make up an oral tradition. In studying the Kanuri people, however, scholars have had a great advantage, for the Kanuri compiled their oral history into what became known as the "Bornu Chronicle." It is true that the chronicle includes the imaginative mythology of the Kanuri, but it is still most informative. We know, for example, that about

A.D. 800, Dugu, the first king of the Sefuwa dynasty, ruled over Kanuri, and that Houmé, who ascended the throne in 1085, was the first Muslim ruler of the empire. The chronicle tells us that by the beginning of the thirteenth century Islam was so well established that Kanem was not only very much a part of the Arab world, but also was the crossroads of trade between the peoples of the Nile and the African countries both south and west of Chad, from the Indian Ocean to the shores of the Gulf of Guinea.

The Kanem Empire reached the peak of its power under King Salma, who ruled from 1194 to 1221. During the hundred years that followed, however, the state was plagued by wars. The Bulala, living to the east of Lake Chad, created such disturbances by their raids that in 1386 Omar, the ruling Mai, or king, moved his people to the western shore of the lake. Bornu, as the new settlement was called, grew to be the most picturesque empire of the medieval Sudan.

The Bornu Empire was ruled much like that of Kanem. Its king continued to be looked upon as a god and was never seen by his subjects; Islam remained the state religion and the laws of the Koran were observed as the laws of the land.

In 1476, Mai Ali ascended the throne. During his twenty-one-year reign, Bornu became a prosperous kingdom. But Mai Ali is best remembered for having built the empire's impressive capital at Berni Gazargamo. The walled city, about one and three-quarter miles in diameter, was certainly one of, if not, the largest African cities of this period. It was located in northern Bornu on the Tobe River, which forms one of the boundary lines of modern Nigeria and Niger; and to this day, the remains of Mai Ali's red brick palace can be seen.

The most famous king of Bornu, however, was Idris

Alooma. He created an army with splendor and pageantry hitherto unknown in Africa. Like the knights of Europe, his soldiers were clad in iron helmets and chain mail, and both soldiers and horses wore heavy quilted coats that served as armor. Men of the Turkish military were brought to Bornu to drill the troops; the army of Bornu boasted of being the first West African army to possess firearms. The strength of Bornu's colorful army was the basis of the empire's prosperity; the wealth of Bornu was dependent upon the prisoners its soldiers captured and sold as slaves.

The empire of Bornu, the most powerful of the states of the central Sudan, lasted until the seventeenth century. With the death of Idris Alooma, in 1617, the great kingdoms of Kanem-Bornu began to decline. "Until then there were no disorders," the Bornu Chronicle records, "the Mai ruled supreme." But after his death, "a civil war broke out and the princes retired each to their different regions."

And so, by the eighteenth century, the great civilizing empire of the central Sudan fell apart—it did not disappear, but merely faded out of the limelight of greatness.

The king of Bornu
receiving visitors.

THE FOREST STATES
(THE NOK AND
YORUBA PEOPLES
AND THE EMPIRE OF BENIN)

The jungles (rain forests) and marshes of western Africa were known to English colonials of the nineteenth century as "the white man's grave." But they were not the only ones who found it virtually impossible to penetrate this area of Africa—few Europeans went beyond the coast before the nineteenth century and Arab travelers found the coastal forest belt equally impenetrable.

The forest states of Africa, therefore, developed quite differently from the states of the Sudan. Living to the south of the grassy plains of the Sudan, the peoples of equatorial Africa differed both physically and culturally from their northern and southern continental brothers.

Neglected by the Arab writers of the Middle Ages, the peoples of the Guinea Coast and the forest states of Africa were long believed by Europeans to be peoples without a history. Today, however, it is clear that their history was not only culturally rich but also politically sophisticated. Though our knowledge is based primarily upon archeological findings and oral tradition, sufficient information exists to piece together a broad picture of the history of this area.

Our first important clue was uncovered in 1936 by a group of tin miners working in central Nigeria. Here, quite by chance, while digging at Jappa, near the village of Nok, some miners unearthed two small red clay heads. We know very little about the "Nok Figurine Culture," as the people who lived at Nok some two millennia ago are now called, but modern scientific methods have proved that these highly artistic lifelike heads were sculpted and baked sometime between 900 B.C. and A.D. 200. Since the unearthing of the first heads, many more artistic pieces have been found; and it appears that the Nok Figurine Culture was spread over some three hundred miles of Nigeria.

Who were the Nok people living on the Nigerian plateau more than two thousand years ago? Were they the ancestors of the Yoruba of modern Nigeria? No one knows, for there is a gap of almost five hundred years in the history of this area.

One link does exist, however, for language experts believe that the mother tongue of the Yoruba could well be three thousand years old. But the Yoruba disagree. They believe there is merit in the medieval Arabic writing that describes "the sons of Kush who marched toward the setting sun." Perhaps the Yoruba were from Kush, or perhaps they were among the peoples who migrated south from Mediterranean Africa sometime during the sixth century. But whatever their origin, by the eighth century the Yoruba were living in western Nigeria and had founded the town of Ife.

Ife, the first of the Yoruba city-states, became the religious and cultural center of Yorubaland. Ife artists worked in the "lost wax" method used by the sculptors of the ancient civilizations of the Nile. They reached incredible heights, perfecting a technique of sculpting that was strongly reminiscent of Nok art. Then, for hundreds of years, their artistic statuary was forgotten. It is only recently that the ancient art of Ife has found its place in

museums around the world; for the statues of Ife rank with the finest bronze, brass, and clay sculpture ever to be made.

Following the founding of Ife, Yorubaland developed rapidly and by A.D. 1000 it was divided into a number of small states. Oyo, which became the most powerful of these states, was on the northern fringe of the forest land. Ife lay within the bounds of the Oyo State; it remained the cultural center of Yorubaland until sometime in the late thirteenth century, when the armies of Oyo conquered the Edo people of Benin, a powerful state to the south of Ife.

According to tradition, the people of Benin share the same early history as the Yoruba. Their legends claim that they are the descendants of the children of Oduduwa, the prince who helped lead the sons of Kush in their journey "toward the setting sun." It is said that, like the Yoruba, they settled at Ife between the sixth and eighth centuries A.D., but their stay was a relatively short one. Although exact dates are almost impossible to determine, it is believed that sometime during the early years of the ninth century, a group of Edo hunters migrated from Ife and settled in the Niger delta near the Gulf of Guinea. It is generally accepted that about A.D. 900 these Edo founded the first dynasty of Benin kings.

Under the Ogiso kings, as the rulers of this dynasty were called, the empire of Benin prospered, its boundaries were enlarged, and there was peace and order within the kingdom. Then, sometime around 1140, the reigning king, Owodo, is said to have ordered the execution of a pregnant woman. The people of Benin were so angry at Owodo's injustice that

A terracotta head
of the Nok people.

he was forced to abdicate his throne and was banished from the empire.

Owodo was the last of the Ogiso dynasty of kings. Henceforth a republican form of government was set up in the country. The people elected Evian as their leader, for under Owodo he had proved his administrative ability and had worked to help his people. Evian's rule lasted about thirty years. When he realized he was becoming too old to continue as the leader of Benin, he appointed his son as his successor. The people, however, refused to accept Evian's son. They insisted that in a republican government a ruler should be elected, not appointed.

And so the people of Benin, unhappy with their own rulers, asked the "Oni," or king, of Yoruba to send one of his sons to rule their land. In the year 1170, Prince Oranmiyan was crowned "Oba" of Benin, and thus began a new dynasty of kings that was to last until 1888.

Under Oranmiyan the empire prospered, but he claimed that "Benin was a land of vexation," and after ruling for twelve years, he renounced the throne. He told the people his reason for abdicating was that "only a child born, trained, and educated in the arts and mysteries of the land" should govern the empire. As a result, in 1200, his son Eweka I was made Oba in his stead.

Eweka I's reign marked the beginning of the empire's rise to greatness. Throughout the thirteenth century, Benin continued to expand its boundaries; the government was patterned after that of Yorubaland and law and order prevailed. In the last decade of the century, the ruling Oba,

A bronze figure
of the Ife people.

Oguola (1280–1295), sent to the Oni of Ife for someone to teach the artists of Benin how to cast in brass. According to tradition, the brass smith Iguegha was sent from Ife and was responsible for introducing the brass industry to Benin. Modern methods of dating art work, however, indicate that brass-casting was first introduced to Benin from Ife about 1400.

Historically, the famous bronze-brass statues of the Benin artists are most important, for they afford us a glimpse into the life of this great empire. Instead of writing a chronicle of important events, Benin artists fashioned brass castings to portray their history. The castings also show us that the economy of their empire was based on foreign trade, for brass can only be made with copper, and copper is not found in southern Nigeria. Benin traders, therefore, must have been in close contact with the western Sudan.

By the middle of the sixteenth century, Benin was the largest empire of Guinea, covering an area that stretched across the Niger delta to modern Lagos. But, with the coming of the European slave traders, the trade of the empire shifted to human merchandise. The Portuguese supplied the soldiers of Benin with guns, and the armies of the empire were ordered to capture slaves. As they set out on their mission, the people of the countryside fled to the jungles. By the beginning of the eighteenth century, large areas of southern Nigeria were deserted and the great Benin Empire faded into the pages of history. But stained by the bloodshed and horrors of the slave trade, Benin is, unfortunately, too often

A bronze figure
of an "oni," or king,
of the Ife people.

remembered as the "City of Blood," rather than as a great center of art.

The rise of the Ashanti people of modern Ghana coincided in time with the rise of Benin. Sometime during the early years of the fifth century, a group of Twi-speaking people known as the Akan settled in the forests of central Guinea. The Akan people, believed to have migrated south from the "great white desert," were divided into over a dozen distinct groups—of these, the Ashanti grew to be the most powerful, and at present this group ranks as the most numerous of the Akans in modern Ghana. The Akan chiefs, like the Yoruba, organized small states, and like the kingdom of Oyo, the original political capital of the Ashanti-Akans, Kumsai, grew to be the most powerful of the Akan states.

During the fifteenth and sixteenth centuries, the threat of invasion from neighboring tribes forced the armies of the Ashanti to maintain a constant vigilance. The unity of the Akan states was their only hope of survival, but it was not until the latter years of the seventeenth century that the king of Kumsai, Osei Tutu, succeeded in bringing the Akan chiefs together.

According to legend, Osei Tutu summoned the chiefs in hope of forming one great nation. As soon as he had explained his plan, a beautiful golden stool descended from heaven and came to rest upon the great leader's knees. The Ashanti,

A bronze figure of a horseman of the Benin people. This figure was an altarpiece in an ancestral shrine of the sixteenth century.

believing that the gods had sent the stool, proclaimed Osei Tutu the "Asantahene," or king, of the new Ashanti Nation.

To the Ashanti, the sacred golden stool contained the soul of their nation; it became the symbol of their country's safety and, like a great force binding the Ashanti together, it helped their nation become the most powerful of the Guinea states.

The Ashanti Nation grew to be very rich primarily because of the gold deposits in their forests. At first their trade was primarily with the peoples of the Sudan, but as their nation expanded westward, they began trading with the coastal tribes who were in direct contact with European merchants. The more powerful the Ashanti became, the more they wanted to eliminate any middlemen; they wanted to make their bargains directly with the European traders. And so the Ashanti army began their merciless slaughter of the coastal peoples, earning a reputation as the most bloodthirsty army in western Africa.

Throughout the nineteenth century, the Ashanti fought to keep the British government from gaining control of their lands. But in 1902, they were finally defeated; the Akan states were forced to become a protectorate of the British Empire and formed a part of Britain's Gold Coast Colony until 1965.

The slave trade was without a doubt a disruptive force in western Africa, and though a few coastal states prospered from the booming trade, it caused the decline of the trans-Saharan trade route and, in fact, helped cause the disin-

A Benin bronze pitcher
in the form of a leopard.
A sixteenth-century piece.

tegration of many West African empires. The slave trade appears to be, although indirectly, partially responsible for the creation of the kingdom of Bushongo.

In 1483, the Portuguese reached the Congo River and established trade relations with the kingdom of Kongo. At the same period, the Kuba people, living in the forests to the north of Kongo, fled southeastward into the grassy woodlands of central Africa. How much the arrival of the Portuguese contributed to the flight of the Kuba is still uncertain, for we know little of the early history of the Kuba, other than that they were a peaceful people. After fleeing from their homeland, they settled near the Kwango River, but in the early years of the seventeenth century, neighboring tribes began to raid their lands. Rather than fight, the Kuba moved further east, settling in the heart of the Congo along the middle Kasai River. Here the Kuba set up their own state, which they named Bushongo in honor of the most respected clan of their tribe. Isolated from both European and Asian influence, the kingdom of Bushongo developed its own distinct culture and became a highly organized and unified state.

Sometime during the early years of the seventeenth century, another clan of Kuba, led by Shamba Bolongongo, invaded Bushongo, killed the reigning king, and took over the kingdom. Though Bolongongo had taken the throne by force, he was a remarkable man and in the stories handed down from generation to generation, King Shamba Bolongongo is described as: "A King whose only conquests were in the field of thought, public prosperity, and social progress."

The kingdom of Bushongo prospered under Bolongongo. According to tradition, he taught the Kuba the art of carv-

62

*Brass weights used
by the Ashanti
for weighing gold.*

ing. If this is true, he was an outstanding teacher, for the wooden and ivory statues carved in Bushongo during the seventeenth century rank with the finest statuary of Ife and Benin.

East of the kingdom of Bushongo, on the borders of the forests of north-central Africa, lived the Bacwezi people. Though they were not really a forest people, their pattern of development was in many ways similar to the peoples of the more truly forest states. Their kingdom rose during the Middle Ages, and until the end of the nineteenth century neither Asian nor European traders had penetrated their lands. Isolated from foreign influence, their states, like the kingdom of Bushongo, were organized on the basis of their own needs and experience.

Though written records are lacking, ancient Ugandan monuments testify to the fact that there is some truth behind the stories of the great Bacwezi kings—giants, it is said, "who wandered without fear or difficulty to places where no man had ever been before." Ugandan legends describe the Bacwezi as a fair people; and it is believed that they originally lived in the area of modern Ethiopia, having migrated south sometime during the fourteenth century. Stories of their remarkable feats seem to indicate that they had no difficulty establishing themselves as a ruling class.

The Bacwezi ruled southern Uganda from A.D. 1300 to 1500. They centralized the government and probably had a number of vassal states under them, for as many as eighteen earthwork sites have been found in western Uganda that have been identified as royal dwellings of Bacwezi kings; furthermore, protective trenches still remain intact, indicating the areas in which the king's great herds of cattle were contained. The Bacwezi were master builders. They constructed dams and built spectacular earth fortresses with trenches as much as six and one-half miles long.

According to the stories of modern Ugandans, the Bacwezi were originally revered as gods. As their powers grew, they became greedy and wanted to benefit from the wealth of their kingdom—Kitara. Once the people of Kitara realized that the Bacwezi were only human, their ruling days were over.

By 1500 the Bacwezi had disappeared. No one was certain from where they had come and, according to legend, they simply vanished from the land. There is, however, a strong possibility that they were the ancestors of the modern Bahima. The Bahima are also a very tall people whose nomadic wanderings are determined by where they find good grazing lands for their cattle.

At about the same time as the Bacwezi disappeared, another group of northerners, the Luo, appeared on the scene. The Luo must have been a well-organized people, for their influence spread rapidly and within a short period of time, they reorganized Kitara into four kingdoms: Bunyoro, Buganda, Toro, and Busogo.

Throughout the seventeenth century the kingdom of Bunyoro, the most powerful of the states, succeeded in gaining control of all of western Uganda. By the eighteenth century, however, Buganda conquered her sister state of Bunyoro. Due to her efficient government, Buganda became—and has retained her position as—the largest and most powerful state in Uganda.

The land of Zanj holds a special place in Africa's history, for it was in memory of the men of Zanj that Dr. Louis Leakey named *Zinjanthropus* man. Although the land of Zanj usually referred to the coast of East Africa from Somalia to northern Mozambique, the word *Zenj* does not mean "coastal"; it is believed to have come from a similar Persian word meaning "black." It is understandable that the ancients limited the word *Zenj* to mean the black men of the east coast of Africa, because these were the only people with whom they had contact. Although Dr. Leakey's finds in the Olduvai Gorge were some four hundred miles inland, he apparently felt his *Zinjanthropus* lived near enough to the land of Zanj to be described as a "man of Zenj."

There is a tremendous gap in our knowledge of how civilization developed from the days of early Stone Age man to the advanced culture that existed two thousand years ago on the east coast of Africa.

From the writings of a Greek merchant, we know that the coastal cities of eastern Africa were trading with Arabia and India at least as early as 500 B.C. The author, possibly a man named Bernice, lived in one of the ports of the Red Sea. About A.D. 120 he wrote *Periplus of the Erythraean Sea,* a guide to the northwest Indian Ocean. The writer described how Arab merchants sailed to the coastal cities of East Africa, which they referred to collectively as the empire of Azania. Here they found rhinoceros horn and tortoiseshell, and here also they sold cotton cloth from India and glassware from Arabia. The writer described the beautiful black African women whom the Arab traders married and the life they led once they settled along the coast. The Arabs learned the original Bantu language spoken on the east coast, but in time it became a mixture of Bantu and Arabic, with many words whose roots can be traced to other languages. The Arabs called the people of Zanj "Swahili," from the Arabic root *Sahil*, or "coast"; eventually the word referred to the language of Zanj, the predominant tongue spoken on the coast.

It is difficult to imagine that almost one thousand years ago prospering cities with great markets were flourishing along the coast of East Africa. These ports of trade extended from the Horn, at the Gulf of Aden, 2,500 miles south to the southern border of modern Mozambique. Great trading vessels from China anchored in these busy ports, and African merchants carried on business with traders from Persia, India, Burma, and Siam. Many of the ports of Zanj were large enough to be called city-states, or even city-empires, for they were independent politically, had their own coinage, and controlled the trade of the hinterland.

Until the twelfth century, African traders living in the seaports located in what is modern Mozambique sold the Asian world its major supply of gold. They acted as middlemen, bringing Arabian cotton to the tribes of the interior in exchange for their gold, obtained from the mines located in the south of modern Rhodesia. As the town of Kilwa, on the coast of modern Tanzania, grew in strength, however, its

*Chinese sailing ships
of the kind that
sailed to Africa.*

merchants sought to corner the market. By the middle of the century Kilwa had a virtual monopoly of the gold trade.

Malindi and Mombassa, both ports on the coast of modern Kenya, were also important trading centers, as was Sofala, a port in what is today Mozambique. The iron mined in the mountains near Sofala, as well as the iron found in the surroundings of Malindi and Mombassa, was used throughout Arabia and India. "The Indians prized African iron," the traders said, "because it was superior to the iron of their own land; it was plentiful, easily worked and of high quality."

The island of Zanzibar, which means the coast of the Zanj, was also an important center of trade. Sailors from Java and Sumatra as well as India and China came to the ports of Zanzibar in search of ivory and gold, which was brought to Zanzibar from the coastal cities of East Africa.

From the eleventh century on, when Muslim traders began to settle along the east coast, the influence of the Arab world became apparent. Mosques were built in every port and Arabic script was adopted in writing Swahili. But the culture of Zanj remained African.

By the fourteenth century, the coastal cities, known as

Over: Left Above: A plan of the
town and fort of Mombassa.
Left Below: A plan of the fort at Sofala.
Right Above: Zanzibar from the sea.
Right Below: Shipping on
the eastern coast of Africa.

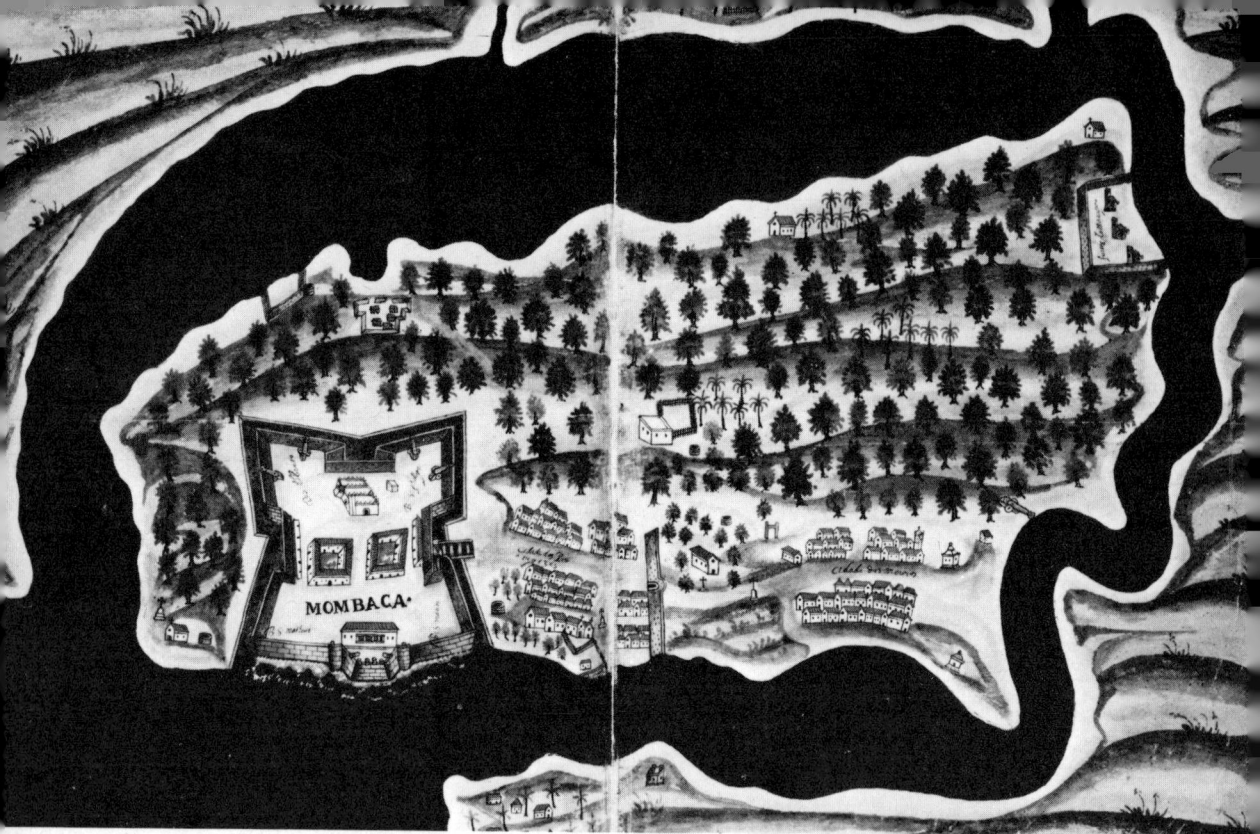

MOMBACA.

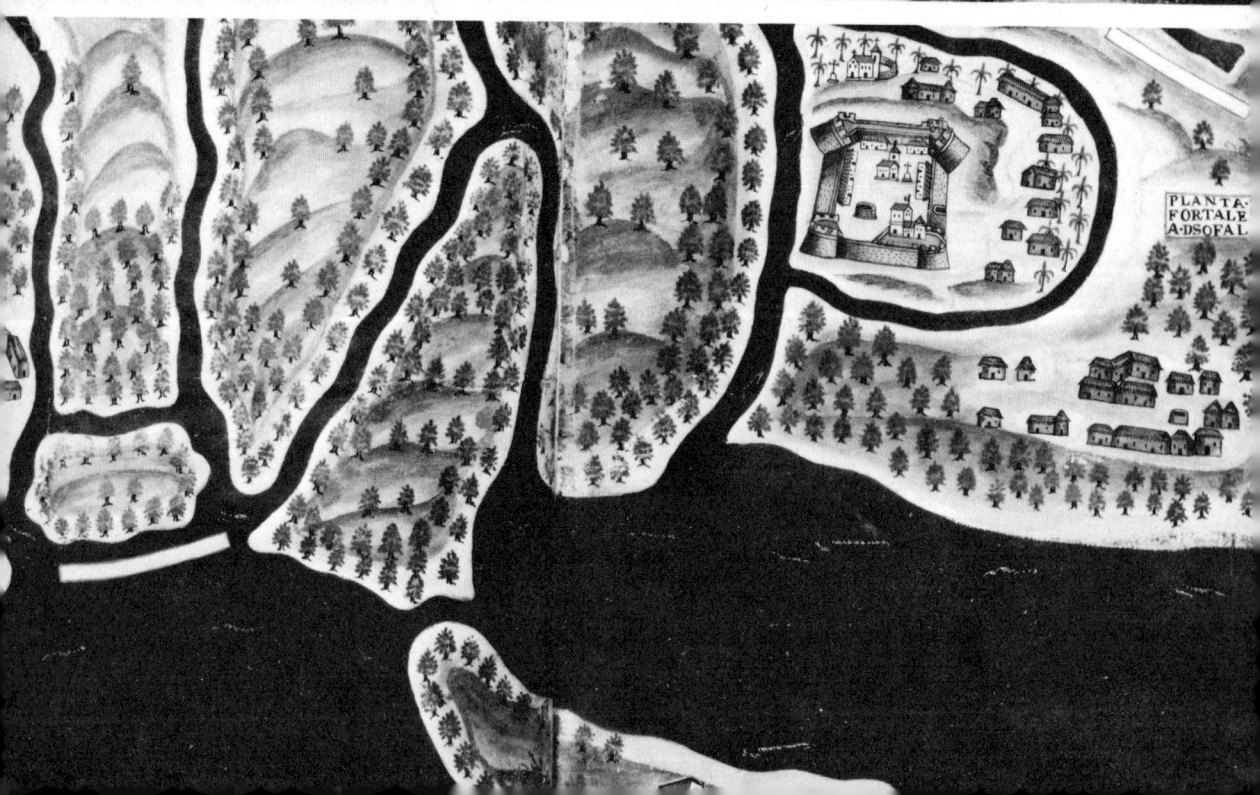

PLANTA FORTALE A DSOFAL

the empire of Zanj, were truly cosmopolitan centers. Kilwa was described as one of the "most beautiful, well-constructed towns in the world." Today, Kilwa is a tiny village, but on a cliff above the town, ruins of a great stone fortress testify to the important position the port once held. And Kilwa was only one of many. In this period also, a hundred years before Europeans had mastered the art of sailing a twin-masted vessel, 2,000-ton Chinese ships, sailing four to seven masts, were anchoring off the eastern coast of Africa. There are even records of one fleet that carried more than 27,000 Chinese to the shores of Zanj.

Then, in 1497, the glorious days of the land of Zanj ended abruptly. On his search for a sea route to India the Portuguese sailor Vasco da Gama reached the exotic ports of Zanj. Following his voyage, other Portuguese pirate-adventurers rounded the tip of South Africa. One by one they attacked and robbed the magnificent cities of the coast, and in so doing, they smashed the trade routes of the Indian Ocean.

From 1500 on, the Chinese stopped sending out any sailing vessels and, though as yet we are still uncertain as to why, they even shut down their shipyards and destroyed all their ships.

The guns and looting of the Portuguese did to the busy seaports of East Africa what the slave trade had done to West Africa. By the seventeenth century, the empire of Zanj was destroyed; all that remained were the Swahili writings of the glories that once were and the dream of what may one day be again.

12

THE GREAT ZIMBABWE

More than fifteen hundred years ago, the Bantu living in eastern Nigeria and central Cameroon began migrating southeastward into the Congo basin and then across the entire southeastern area of the continent. They were not a single group, but rather many peoples speaking related languages who are believed to have originated in the same area.

The Bantu migrations, which probably began during the fourth or fifth century A.D., were to a great extent made possible because of the coming of the Iron Age to sub-Saharan Africa. As the Bantu began pushing southward, through the equatorial forests, they encountered the Mbuti Pygmy. The Pygmy, a people whose maximum height is about 4′6″, were still living a simple life, concerned primarily with hunting. They were afraid of the Bantu, who were armed with iron-tipped spears, and many fled into the depths of the jungles. There were, however, Pygmy who befriended the Bantu, becoming their guides and acting as their scouts. When the Bantu reached the southern part of the continent, they encountered another group of hunters, the Bushmen. Like the Pygmy, the Bushmen are also short, rarely growing taller than 5′2″, and like the Pygmy, the Bushmen who feared the newcomers also fled—they, however, were driven southward into the Kalahari Desert;

those who remained were gradually absorbed into the more advanced Bantu community.

The Iron Age did not suddenly replace Stone Age civilization. Techniques of mining and smelting developed gradually, but as the use of iron spread, it virtually created a cultural revolution. During the first millennium A.D., before the Bantu had acquired a knowledge of how to mine and smelt iron, they had lived in scattered groups and their very existence had depended upon how skillfully they hunted and how fortunate they were in finding wild fruits and vegetables. Once, however, they began to hunt with iron-tipped spears and arrows and were able to cultivate the land with iron tools, their pattern of living changed significantly. They gave up their nomadic existence and began to form communal settlements. The use of the iron-tipped spear as a weapon was an important step leading to tribal organization, for well-armed clans with leadership and discipline soon found they could conquer and absorb weaker groups.

As the Bantu perfected their methods of fashioning tools, they were able to improve their methods of farming; they discovered that by terracing hillsides they were able to conserve the soil and at the same time to irrigate the land. The result was that their food supply increased substantially. No longer faced with the same difficult problems of survival, their population began to increase rapidly. This "population explosion" had a significant effect upon African history, for to this day, the Bantu form the major portion of the population in southeast Africa.

The Bantu migrations took place in three successive waves, lasting over a period of seven hundred years. The earliest group, believed to be the direct ancestors of the modern Shona-speaking people of Rhodesia, settled along

74

the northern banks of the Zambezi River between the fourth and sixth centuries A.D. They chose a site about seventeen miles southeast of Fort Victoria for their royal village, and here, it is believed, they built the earliest "zimbabwe." The word *zimbabwe* is derived from two Bantu words: *zimba,* meaning "houses," and *mabgi,* meaning "stone."

Sometime during the latter years of the eleventh century, a new wave of Shona-speaking Bantu, later known as the Karange, moved into the area. It is believed that the Karange had lived some two hundred miles to the south of Zimbabwe, in an area with rich gold fields. For at least a hundred years they had been mining gold and supplying the traders of the ports of Zanj with the precious metal. When their salt supplies began to run out, however, they were forced to move to an area where they could obtain this vitally important dietary supplement. The Karange apparently encountered no resistance when they took over Zimbabwe and henceforth established their own capital on the earlier Shona site. The Karange capital, which became known as the Great Zimbabwe, was the largest and most impressive of the royal stone cities in Africa and flourished until the beginning of the nineteenth century.

Tribal stories, together with scientific dating methods, enable us to know that the Great Zimbabwe was not built during one period, but rather evolved over a number of centuries, the earliest remains dating back more than a thousand years. The buildings of Zimbabwe were designed in rounded fashion, and their gracefully curving walls seemed to be patterned after the circular mud huts so common throughout the Bantu communities in southeast Africa.

During the early years of the fifteenth century, Monomotapa, the greatest king of the Karange, ruled the empire of

Zimbabwe. He was considered a god by the inland kingdoms of East Africa, and his people not only bowed before him, but also actually crawled on their stomachs to approach him. Monomotapa was not only an able ruler, but also a great warrior. Sometime around 1425, he decided to extend his rule over the whole gold-bearing region between the Zambezi and the Limpopo rivers and then eastward through modern Mozambique, in order to have access to the coastal ports of trade. It was probably this desire to have a great empire that accounted for the fact that during his reign an extensive building program of the capital was started and the Great Zimbabwe was greatly enlarged. By the middle of the century, Monomotapa's powerful kingdom, which became known by his name, extended from the Zambezi River to the Indian Ocean and stretched seven hundred miles across Southern Rhodesia to the northern borders of modern Transvaal.

The most outstanding structures of Monomotapa's capital were the hilltop fortress, known as the "Acropolis," and the temple or palace, which stood on the plain below the fort. The buildings, made of local granite, were not only masterpieces of architectural achievement but today are also considered among the wonders of the world. The builders used neither mortar nor mud in their constructions; they relied solely upon balance and the skill of their masons. The granite was cut to perfection and complicated patterns were worked into the walls. The temple covered an area of 292 feet in length and 220 feet in width. It was not a single struc-

Above: A model of the ruins of Zimbabwe.
Below: A ruined tower of Zimbabwe.

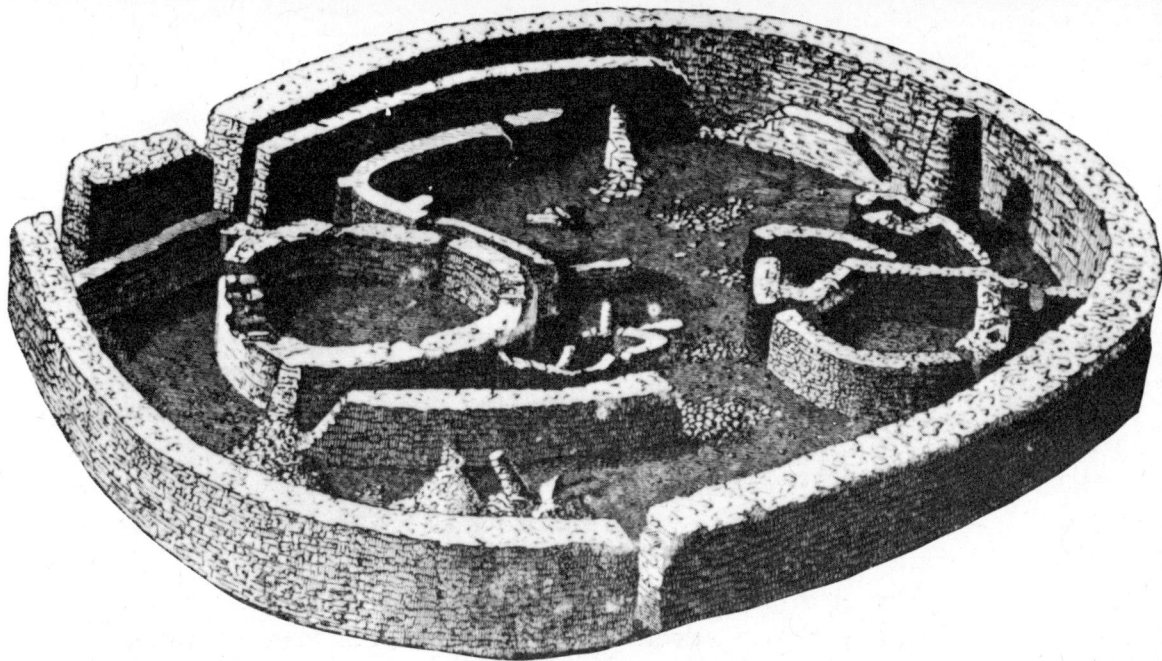

ture, but rather several buildings connected by a maze of walled passages. At the top of the temple wall, which in places was 30 feet high and 14 feet thick, a double chevron pattern was worked into the granite. This triangular design signified that the building was the residence of the king. A great conical tower rose above the temple walls, reaching a height of more than 34 feet. The builders of the Acropolis made the most of the terrain. They built the imposing structure into the granite rock of the hillside so that it towered some 200 feet above the temple. Scientists have determined that the construction of the great fortress was still in progress as recently as the middle of the eighteenth century.

The great stone city of Zimbabwe was the capital of the Karange, but it was not the only town built out of granite rock. More than three hundred such cities have been found throughout Rhodesia and Mozambique.

The vast empire of Monomotapa lasted until the beginning of the seventeenth century, when another group of Shona-Bantu, the Rozwi, tried to overthrow the kingdom. The internal rivalry between the Karange and the Rozwi was the major factor leading to the decline of Monomotapa's empire. In an attempt to retain their independence, the people of Monomotapa turned to the Portuguese, who by this time were well established along the coast. The Portuguese promised to protect them, but in reality, their only interest was in finding the internal source of Zimbabwe's gold and capturing inland people whom they could sell as slaves. The Monomotapa eventually fled to the south; their subject kingdoms deserted them, giving their allegiance to the Rozwi, and the Monomotapa were left at the mercy of their Portuguese overlords.

The powerful Zimbabwe Empire of the Rozwi, free from

Portuguese influence, continued to prosper. Further building was carried out at the site of the Great Zimbabwe, and soapstone carvings were added to the top of the walls to enhance the structures.

Unfortunately, few written records have been found describing the great Shona cultures of the empires of Zimbabwe-Monomotapa and Rozwi. In the sixteenth century, the Portuguese traveled up the Zambezi River to the empire of Monomotapa, where they saw a number of cities of these "stone-building" people; but the empire where the Rozwi ruled remained beyond their reach, and until 1840, when the empire collapsed, no foreigner had seen the greatest of the stone cities of Africa's interior kingdoms, the Great Zimbabwe.

When the ruins of the Great Zimbabwe were first discovered, scholars doubted their origin as being African. Today, there is no doubt that this royal city, together with the other stone cities of the interior, were designed and built by the Shona-Bantu of southern Africa; they alone were the architects of the Zimbabwe.

There are many gaps in the history of black Africa, but even a brief glimpse of the empires that once flourished across the vast continent reveals the greatness of Africa's heritage.

Archeologists are continually searching for new evidence, digging for ruins that will help illuminate the story of Africa's past; and linguists are patiently looking for clues that will help to decipher ancient languages such as the "Meroitic cursive script" written in the kingdom of Kush.

But even with the limited knowledge at hand, we know that the history of the black African empires is one of noble kings and mighty warriors; it is a story of vast empires with highly centralized governments; of cities such as Jenné and Timbuktu, which were great centers of learning; and others, such as Ife and Benin, whose claim to fame was through their art.

It is too often forgotten that the civilizations of Africa have always been a part of the stream of world history. Ignorance alone is the only excuse for those who maintain that Africa is a continent without a history. It is true that the story of black Africa's past has been neglected. Now the time has come when people everywhere should learn from the age-old African proverb: "Not to know is bad, not to wish to know is worse."

BIBLIOGRAPHY

Ajayi, A.F.A., and Crowder, Michael. *History of West Africa*. London, Nigeria: Longman Group Ltd., 1971.

Brooks, Lester. *Great Civilizations of Ancient Africa*. New York: Four Winds Press, 1971.

————. *Old Africa Rediscovered*. London: Victor Gollancz Ltd., 1961.

————. *Africa in History*. London: Weidenfeld & Nicolson, 1968.

Hollingsworth, L. W. *A Short History of the East Coast of Africa*. London: Macmillan & Co. Ltd., 1949.

Levtzion, Nehemia. *Ancient Ghana and Mali*. London: Methuen & Co., Ltd., 1973.

Maquet, Jacques. *Civilizations of Black Africa*. London: Oxford University Press, 1972.

Oliver, Roland, and Fage, J. D. *A Short History of Africa*. London: Penguin Books Ltd., 1962.

INDEX

Songhai, 40–42, 43
Waterworks:
    dams of Bacwezi, 65
    reservoirs of Kush, 19
Weapons:
    Bornu, 49
    guns introduced by Europeans, 57, 72
    iron, 16, 22, 49, 73
    Songhai, 43
West Africa:
    Arab influences in, 11–14, 22, 25, 26,
      35
    forest states of, 50–64 (*see also*
      Ashanti; Benin; Ife)
    skin coloring, 5
    slave trade, 57, 61–62, 72
Western Sudan:

empire of Ghana, 21–29, 38, 40
empire of Mali, 31–37, 38, 40, 46
Songhai Empire extended to, 42
Wood carvings, Bushongo, 64
Writing:
    Arabic, 69
    Meroitic cursive, 19, 81

Yoruba people, 51, 53, 54, 58. *See also*
    Ife; Oyo

Za el Ayamen, king of Songhai, 38
Zambesi River, 75, 76, 79
Zanj, 2, 66–72, 75
Zanzibar, 69
Zimbabwe, kingdoms of, 75–79
Zinjanthropus, 2, 11, 66

ABOUT
THE AUTHOR

Joan Joseph is a graduate
of McGill University
and has studied at the
University of Southern California,
the Université d'Aix-Marseille,
and the University of Paris.
She holds a foundation grant
for historical research
on thirteenth-century England,
which she is presently
pursuing in London.
Joan Joseph is the author
of several books
for young people,
including *Henry Hudson*.